OTHER HELEN EXLEY GIFTBOOKS IN THIS SERIES:

Over 30's Jokes   A Spread of Over 40's Jokes
A Triumph of Over 50's Jokes   A Jubilee of Over 60's Jokes
Over 70's Jokes   Old Wrecks Jokes'
A Chuckle of Kids Jokes   A Romp of Naughty Jokes

Published in 1990 by Helen Exley Giftbooks in Great Britain.
Selection and arrangement copyright © Helen Exley 1990
Cartoons copyright © Bill Stott 1990
The moral right of the author has been asserted.

12 11 10 9 8 7 6 5 4 3 2

Cartoons by Bill Stott.
Assistant Editor: Samantha Armstrong.
Series Editor: Helen Exley.

ISBN: 978-1-84634-228-8

Acknowledgements: Jokes by Robert McCune are reproduced by kind permission of Angus and
Robertson Publishers. IMPORTANT COPYRIGHT NOTICE: PAM BROWN, PETER GRAY,
BILL STOTT, HELEN THOMPSON © HELEN EXLEY 1990.

Helen Exley Giftbooks, 16 Chalk Hill, Watford, Herts WD19 4BG, UK.
www.helenexleygiftbooks.com

A ROUND OF
GOLF
JOKES

CARTOONS BY
BILL STOTT

H E L E N   E X L E Y

Golf: "A game in which one endeavors to control a ball with implements ill adapted for the purpose."

WOODROW WILSON

●

Golf Ball: A small object that remains on the tee while a perspiring citizen fans it vigorously with a large club.

●

"If you are going to throw a club, it is important to throw it ahead of you, down the fairway, so you don't waste energy going back to pick it up."

TOMMY BOLT

●

Local rule at the Nyanza Golf Club: "If a ball comes to rest in dangerous proximity to a hippopotamus or crocodile, another ball may be dropped at a safe distance, no nearer the hole, without penalty."

●

"MR. FINNINGTON — ALMOST ANYONE CAN LEARN TO PLAY GOLF,
UNFORTUNATELY — YOU'RE AN ALMOST."

"The entire handbook can be reduced to three rules.
One: you do not touch your ball from the time you tee
it up to the moment you pick it out of the hole. Two:
don't bend over when you are in the rough. Three:
when you are in the woods, keep clapping your hands."

CHARLES PRICE, from *Esquire*

"What's the matter?" Charlie asked impatiently. Charlie and Jim were teeing off but Jim was rather a long time taking his stance.

"My wife came along today — she's watching me now from the clubhouse, and I want to make this next shot a good one," Jim explained.

"Good Lord," Charlie exploded, "you haven't got a hope of hitting her at this distance."

ROBERT McCUNE, from *The World's Best Golf Jokes*

"The hardest shot is a mashie at ninety yards from the green, where the ball has to be played against an oak tree, bounces back into a sandtrap, hits a stone, bounces on the green and then rolls into the cup. That shot is so difficult I have only made it once."

ZEPPO MARX

"He enjoys that perfect peace, that peace beyond all understanding, which comes at its maximum only to the man who has given up golf."

P.G. WODEHOUSE

"NO AUDREY I WILL NOT CONCEDE. NOW HOLD THAT TORCH STEADY"

For months the archaeologists had been toiling deep in the Amazon jungle, clearing creepers and rampant, choking undergrowth from faint traces of a Lost City. Their excitement mounted as the place's extraordinary purpose became evident. Broad, winding avenues of giant flagstones had deep, narrow, perfectly circular holes every few hundred yards. It had to be . . . a golf course! Any doubt was dispelled by the discovery of stone panels depicting human figures using primitive prototypes of irons or putters.

Next step was to interrogate local Indian tribesmen about traditions associated with the prehistoric golf club. And yes, the tribes did have legends of Old Ones who followed a daily ritual with clubs and balls, until routed by tragedy. Watching a particularly wrinkled, aged elder chattering to the interpreter, a Professor murmured wistfully, "If only we knew why they gave up golf, making it vanish for centuries before rediscovery."

The interpreter nodded eagerly and relayed the query. The elder, surprised, made a sweeping gesture at the jungle, and replied tersely. "Simple," was the translation, "they couldn't afford the green fees."

●

During the club's annual dinner, one member had much too little blood in his alcohol stream. He grew increasingly restive as the guest speaker droned on and on. Finally, the infuriated drunk picked up a bottle, weaved around behind the top table, and swung a savage blow at the unstoppable orator.

Unfortunately, he clobbered the club captain. "Hit me again," the victim pleaded, disappearing under the table, "I can still *hear* the swine!"

●

"AS A NEW MEMBER, YOU OUGHT TO KNOW THAT YOU ALWAYS SAY 'YES' WHEN THE PRESIDENT'S WIFE WANTS TO PLAY THROUGH . . ."

A Club Secretary strolled out the course a bit to see how a competition in connection with his Club was progressing. He observed a competitor addressing his ball at the fifth hole a yard and a half in front of the tee box, and he at once went up to him and said "You must not do that." "Mind your own business" was the rejoinder. "I'll have you understand," said the Secretary, "it is my duty to see that no competitor infringes the rules, and if you hit that ball you are ipso facto disqualified." The competitor ceased addressing the ball, and turning to the Secretary made the bitter retort, "Can't you mind your own business. I am playing my third!"

ANONYMOUS, from *Told At The 19th Hole*

●

"I have never played on such a course in my life," complained a visitor to his caddie. "You left the course twenty minutes ago, Sir," said the caddie drily. "You're half way ower tae Strathtyrum now."

SCOTTISH GOLFER, from *Humorous St Andrew's Golf Stories*

●

"I'd give up golf if I didn't have so many sweaters."

BOB HOPE

"OH! A KNITTED GOLF GLOVE. HOW THOUGHTFUL."

"THIS REALLY IS MOST SPORTING OF YOU . . ."

When lightning struck: "There was a thunderous crack like cannonfire and suddenly I was lifted a foot and a half off the ground . . . Damn, I thought to myself, this is a helluva penalty for slow play."

LEE TREVINO

It had been one of those days. A jinxed round succeeded in making the scratch golfer look an absolute rabbit. Maddened, he bent a club across his knee, drowned his best putter in the water hazard, shook his fist at the sky and bellowed, "Come down here and fight fair!"

●

Satan, fuming, called a staff meeting. Hades had become too soft an option, he scolded, due to their fiendish complacency and idleness. Every little devil must tighten up, crack down, and give guests a hell of a time, he decreed. "I want them tested to the limit, tormented, humiliated — but the twist is, you must hold out a false promise that things will get better."

"Like it is in golf, eh?" a fork-tailed junior executive suggested, anxious to show he had caught on.

And Satan, taken aback, sputtered, "Hold on, nothing *that* strong, old son. They're only human, and they have to last out for eternity, remember . . ."

●

"My goal this year is basically to find the fairways."

LAURI PETERSON, from the *San Jose Mercury News*

●

Golf: "A game in which a ball one and a half inches in diameter is placed on a ball 8,000 miles in diameter. The object is to hit the small ball but not the larger."

JOHN CUNNINGHAM

The oldest member of our golf club came into the club-house after his usual six holes and complained that he couldn't get out of the bunkers as well as he once could. His listeners suggested a number of possible remedies, but the old man shook his head.

"It's not the ball that troubles me," he explained sadly, "It's getting *myself* out."

MAJOR C. GIBSON

After an abominable round of golf, a man is known to have slit his wrists with a razor blade and, having bandaged them, to have stumbled into the locker room and enquired of his partner, "What time tomorrow?"

ALISTAIR COOKE

"Even when times were good, I realized that my earning power as a golf professional depended on too many ifs and putts."

GENE SARAZEN, from *Thirty Years of Championship Golf*

The world's worst golfer hit his ball into a monstrous bunker.

"What club should I use now?" he wailed to his caddie.

"What club you use isn't important," answered the young man.

"Just take along plenty of food and water."

STEVE KEUCHEL

●

"In the club-house at a course quite near to Chepstow, you can see the first tee and by swivelling the head slightly, the eighteenth green. As one member put it occasional excitement one side, regular comedy at the other."

BILL STOTT

●

Ruining yet another shot, the duffer whimpered, "There can't be worse players than me."

"There are," his partner assured him, "but they're no longer playing."

●

To his pupil: "You've just one problem. You stand too close to the ball — after you've hit it."

SAM SNEAD

"LET'S TRY SOMETHING ELSE MR SPONSWICK, THE HOLDING THE BREATH TRICK'S NOT WORKING . . ."

Dentist: "Gee, Mrs Bellamy, I'm sorry. Try the emergency dental clinic up in Main Street. Cross my heart, I have eighteen cavities to fill this afternoon. I have no time before making a start."

Dental Nurse: "Don't forget to take your new putter, Mr Adams."

J. R. COULSON

●

Irked by Peter Putter's request for yet another day off, to attend the funeral of his fifth or sixth grandmother — death always struck the family during the Open — the boss grumbled, "I wish you cared as much about your work as you do about golf."

Shocked into truthfulness, Pete admitted, "No way, I could never take work *that* seriously."

●

"Give me golf clubs, fresh air and a beautiful partner, and you can keep my golf clubs and the fresh air."

JACK BENNY

●

"He took a swing like a man with a wasp under his shirt and his pants on fire, trying to impale a butterfly on the end of a scythe."

PAUL GALLICO, from *Golf Is a Nice Friendly Game*

Too many golfers grip the club at address like they were trying to choke a prairie coyote to death.

CURT WILSON

"HE USES GOLF TO UNWIND..."

Robinson Crusoe style, the shipwrecked golfer made the best of his tiny island. When a cruise liner spotted his distress signals and sent a boat to investigate, the landing party was amazed to find a crude but recognizable nine-hole course which the castaway had played with driftwood woods, whalebone and coral putter and balls carved out of pumice stone.

"Quite a layout," said the officer in charge of the rescuers.

"Too kind, it's very rough and ready," the goatskin-clad golfer responded. Then he smiled slyly. "But I am quite proud of the water hazard . . . "

●

"Sneaky little devil, Polts. Thought he was just a terrible player . . . . But he's laid a lawn front and back of his new bungalow, entirely out of divots."

J. R. COULSON

●

The latest statistical survey of golfers' height, conducted on behalf of a major sportswear company, reveals that the average player is seldom as tall as his stories.

●

"WELL — THEY'RE NOT DOING ANY HARM AND THEY'VE PROMISED TO
TIDY UP — LATER."

"THAT'S THE PRIZELLIS — DELIGHTFUL COUPLE.

CIRCUS BACKGROUND APPARENTLY."

"The devoted golfer is an anguished soul who has learned a lot about putting just as an avalanche victim has learned a lot about snow."

DAN JENKINS, from *The Dogged Victims of Inexorable Fate*

●

When ground rules permit a golfer to improve his lie, he can either move his ball or change the story about his score.

●

"At first a golfer excuses a dismal performance by claiming bad lies. With experience, he covers up with better ones."

P. BROWN

●

A friend who had a powerful telescope, invited Old Tom Morris to make use of it for a view of the moon. Tom looked at the magnified moon attentively. "Faith, sir," he said, "she's terrible full o' bunkers."

from *Told at the 19th Hole*

●

"Every day I try to tell myself this is going to be fun today. I try to put myself in a great frame of mind before I go out — then I screw it up with the first shot."

JOHNNY MILLER, from *Golf Magazine*, 1984

●

"Mildred, shut up" cried the golfer at his nagging wife. "Shut up or you'll drive me out of my mind."

"That," snapped Mildred, "wouldn't be a drive. That would be a putt."

ROBERT McCUNE, from *The World's Best Golf Jokes*

●

Very proud of having walked around with him for the first time, Daddy's Little Angel couldn't wait to tell everyone about it. "My father is the best golfer in the whole world," she claimed "He can play for hours and hardly ever lets the ball go into those little holes."

●

"JUST THINK — IF YOU HAD BEEN STANDING SEVEN YARDS TO THE LEFT, THAT WOULD'VE BEEN A MATCH WINNER!"

The difference between learning to play golf and learning to drive a car is that in golf you never hit anything.

"It's that you lose *nerves*, not nerve. You can shoot lions in the dark and yet you can quiver like a leaf and fall flat over a two-foot putt."

JOHNNY FARRELL

●

The headmaster was presiding at his school's Sports Day, while a celebrity guest waited to present prizes. The head droned through his standard set of clichés about parallels between sport and adult life awaiting his pupils. Sportsmanship was precious, he said, and would earn success and respect in every sort of job, just as it did in any sport the boys could imagine.

"Obviously not a golfer," thought the VIP.

●

"If you watch a game, it's fun. If you play it, it's recreation. If you work at it, it's golf."

BOB HOPE

●

Real golfers don't cry when they line up their fourth putt.

KAREN HURWITZ

●

"LOOK AT THE WAY IT'S LOOKING AT ME. IT KNOWS I HATE IT."

"LOOK — IF YOU'RE GOING TO HESITATE ABOUT MARRYING ME,
WE'D BETTER LET THEM PLAY THROUGH . . ."

"What is Love compared with holing out before your opponent?"

P. G. WODEHOUSE, from *Archibald's Benefit*

Tempted to embark on yet another extra marital affair, Bill was absent-mindedly reviewing the situation to himself in the bar.

"Not worth it," he muttered. "Never as good as you hoped. Expensive. Drives the wife berserk."

His friend, who happened to overhear his soliloquy, leaned across.

"Come now, old son. You knew what to expect when you took up golf."

P. BROWN

●

"You think so much of your old golf game that you don't even remember when we were married," complained the wife.

"Of course I do, honey," the husband reassured her. "It was the day after I sank that forty-foot putt."

HERBERT V. PROCHNOW & HERBERT V. PROCHNOW JNR.

●

"You know your husband is obsessed when he thinks The Green Party is something to do with the improvement of golf courses."

J. R. COULSON

Back at the nineteenth, in a vile mood, he delivered his bitter tale of woe.

"Nothing could stop me winning. I had a putt of about eleven inches, hardly more than a tap-in, to clinch it. The green was dead flat, perfectly true, a real billiard table. Not a breath of wind.

"My ball was heading for the cup, on rails. Then a raven swooped down, snatched it up, and circled the flag stick, twice. The raven passed the ball to a vulture, which flapped over to Paradise Brook, opened its talons and . . . splash. End of story."

St. Peter sighed deeply and vowed, "Last time I ever play St. Francis of Assisi."

●

"It's good sportsmanship to not pick up lost golf balls while they are still rolling."

MARK TWAIN

●

Never smash a club over your opponent's head. You can't replace it under the fourteen club rule.

H. THOMSON

●

"I DON'T CARE HOW ORIGINAL IT IS — UNFAIR PLAY IS UNFAIR PLAY."

On the seventeenth, beside a main road, the two friends glanced up to see a funeral cortege passing. One of them dropped his club, whipped off his cap and stood with head bowed in reverent silence until the procession was out of sight. Impressed, his pal remarked, "Good to see old conventions upheld — not many have such good manners, these days."

Replacing his cap, the other man smiled modestly. "Well we were married for twenty-six years."

●

"I've always had a wife — golf. No man should have more than one."

FREDDIE McCLEOD

●

"Why the long face?"
My husband says I must choose between him and golf.
"Sorry to hear it."
Me too — I'm really going to miss him.

●

*"ANOTHER GREAT SHOT DEBBIE! OH DEAR, YOUR HUSBAND HAS
BROKEN HIS DRIVER IN TWO!"*

Niggled by impatience and open hostility in the lengthening line behind him, Wally Wimpe lowered his club, looked back and said haughtily, "I'm entitled to take my time over addressing the ball."

"Quick, somebody remind him where the ball lives," came a weary appeal from the back of the crowd.

●

"DON'T MIND ME — CARRY ON — I'VE GOT TO A GOOD BIT."

"To get an elementary grasp of the game of golf, a human must learn, by endless practice, a continuous and subtle series of highly unnatural movements, involving about sixty-four muscles, that result in a seemingly natural swing, taking all of two seconds to begin and end."

ALISTAIR COOKE

"A member of my husband's golf club raced back to the clubhouse from a lone practice round to announce excitedly, "I've just had a hole in one on the seventeenth — and I've left the ball in the hole to prove it!""

MRS K. PLOWMAN

Advice to a pupil: "Lay off for three weeks and then quit for good."

SAM SNEAD

Give me a man with big hands, big feet and no brains and I will make a golfer out of him.

WALTER HAGEN

"Golfers don't fist fight. They cuss a lot. But they wouldn't punch anything or anybody. They might hurt their hands and have to change their grip."

DAN JENKINS, from *Dead Solid Perfect*, 1974

●

On injuring her foot: "It was stupid. I learned a lesson. When you have a fight with a club, the club always wins."

PATTI HAYES

"SO, YOU CALLED HIM A CHEAT . . . THEN WHAT HAPPENED?"

"DEAR GOD. THANK YOU FOR ENCOURAGING MY WIFE TO TAKE UP GOLF. PLEASE DON'T EVER LET HER GET BETTER THAN ME . . ."

"Love has had a lot of press-agenting from the oldest times; but there are higher, nobler things than love. A woman is only a woman, but a hefty drive is a slosh."

P. G. WODEHOUSE, *A Woman Is Only A Woman*

●

"Can't stand women en masse. Typing pools. Tearing each other to pieces every time a back is turned. Gossip. Jockeying for position. Sulks."

"Odd you should feel that way. I thought you belonged to a Golf Club."

PETER GRAY

●

"A wife always knows when her husband has had a bad round. He has pond weed in his socks."

P. BROWN

●

There was a hold up at the short eleventh hole and just as they were about to play off, a man rushed off the tenth green. "I beg your pardon," he called, "but would you mind very much if I played through? I've just heard that my wife has been taken seriously ill."

●

"The proper score for a businessman golfer is 90. If he is better than that he is neglecting his business. If he's worse, he's neglecting his golf."

ST ANDREW'S ROTARY MEMBER *(18 handicap)*

●

"I don't say my golf game is bad; but if I grew tomatoes, they'd come up sliced."

MILLER BARBER

●

"INGENIOUS BUT SADLY, ILLEGAL TOO."

Few people carry a heavy burden farther than golf caddies.

●

"The best place to refine your swing is, of course, right out on the practice range . . . . You will have an opportunity to make the same mistakes over and over again so that you no longer have to think about them, and they become part of your game."

STEPHEN BAKER, from *How to Play Golf in the Low 120's*

●

"What kind of player is Johnny Bean?" asked one member of his caddie on the day before the competition. "Hopeless. He slices, goes into every bunker. He thinks you get to the hole via the rough." "Great news" said the member. "Not really, sir. He'll beat you."

H.M.E.

●

"YOU are without doubt the worst caddie in the world!"

"Never — that would be too much of a coincidence."

"Real golfers, whatever the provocation, never strike a caddie with the driver. The sand wedge is far more effective."

HUXTABLE PIPPEY

Old Willie, genial soul, liked to encourage the players who employed him as a caddie, by appreciative comments on the strokes they played. One day his "man", expending on a tee stroke more energy and zeal than skilful guidance, essayed a vigorous swing which was just too high to encounter the ball. "That would hae been a splendid shot," chirruped Willie, "if ye had but hit the ball."

from *Told at the 19th Hole*

"When they were awarding a car for a hole-in-one on a certain hole, I hit a four-wood . . . and my ball bounced onto the hood of the car. Someone told me "I don't think you understand. You have to hit the hole, not the car."

MARY DWYER

"The truly great things happen when a genius is alone. This is true especially among golfers."

J. R. COULSON

"Golf, like measles, should be caught young, for, if postponed to riper years, the results may be serious."

P. G. WODEHOUSE, from *A Mixed Threesome*

"NEVER MIND — YOU'RE ON THE GREEN IN TWO . . ."

"I'd like to see the fairways more narrow. Then everybody would have to play from the rough, not just me."

SEVE BALLESTEROS

●

"The trouble that most of us find with the modern matched sets of clubs is that they don't really seem to know any more about the game than the old ones did!"

ROBERT BROWNING, from A History of Golf

●

Horace Hacker showed his usual form — diabolical — and logically enough, was having a game to match. The caddie was teetering toward breaking point… It came after forty strokes or so, at the fifth hole. "What should I take for this one?" Horace asked innocently.

"Beats me," growled the expert. "Seems like a toss-up between a cyanide capsule or the next train out of town!"

●

"Golf and sex are about the only things you can enjoy without being good at it."

JIMMY DEMARET

●

"Golfers find it a very trying matter to turn at the waist, more particularly if they have a lot of waist to turn."

HARRY VARDON

●

"The flags on the greens ought to be at half-staff."

AL MALETESTA, amateur golfer, on his game, *San Francisco Examiner*, 1982.

●

To the comedian, George Burns: "George, you look perfect, . . . that beautiful knitted shirt, an alpaca sweater, those expensive slacks . . . . You've got an alligator bag, the finest matched irons, and the best woods money can buy. It's a damn shame you have to spoil it all by playing golf."

LLOYD MANGRUM

●

"I'M GOOD AT GOLF. I CAN FEEL IT INSIDE ME. IT JUST NEVER COMES OUT WHILE I'M PLAYING."

"Well, in plain old English, I'm driving it bad, chipping bad, putting bad, and not scoring at all. Other than that, and the fact I got up this morning, I guess everything's okay.

BOB WYNN

Golf is a lot of walking, broken up by disappointment and bad arithmetic.

"Golf is a non-violent game played violently from within."

BOB TOSKI

●

"Real golfers go to work to relax".

GEORGE DILLON

●

"AHH! THIS IS THE LIFE . . ."

"I DON'T THINK HE'S A MEMBER BUT I'D LOVE TO KNOW WHERE HE GOT HIS BUGGY."

"How are you getting on with your new clubs?" asked the golfer when he walked into the bar and saw a friend of his. "Fine," replied the friend. "They put twenty yards on my slice."

DAI REES, from *Dai Rees on Golf*, 1959

A young man from St Andrew's was coming along very well, and his handicap had been reduced to scratch, and the fact had gone slightly to his head. He had been telling all and sundry and was ready with the news for old Davie, a professional. "That's a fine bonnet you're wearing," Davie interrupted him, "now and then, take it off and measure it, measure it."

ANONYMOUS, from *Told At The 19th Hole*

●

"Golf appeals to the idiot in us and the child. What child does not grasp the pleasure-principle of miniature golf? Just how childlike golf players become is proven by their frequent inability to count past five."

JOHN UPDIKE

●

"To that man, age brought only golf instead of wisdom."

GEORGE BERNARD SHAW

●

"THERE'S ONE OF THOSE NEW FANGLED GOLF TROLLEYS
WITH A SPOILER — ON BOTH ENDS!"

"Golf is a good walk spoiled."

MARK TWAIN

"If this was a prize fight, they'd stop it."

BOB HOPE

"GOSH IT'S FERNLEY — OBVIOUSLY BEEN ARGUING OVER DROPPED
BALLS AGAIN."

Handicapped golfer: the man playing his boss.

●

The Bishop, elderly, yet still a formidable player, regularly trounced the Rural Dean. "Never mind," the Bishop consoled him, "you have many years in which to improve, and my future is limited — you'll bury me, one day."

"Yes, Bishop . . . but it'll still be your hole."

●

"If the following foursome is pressing you, wave them through and then speed up".

DEANE BEMAN

●

Talking about Vietnam: "There's not as much pressure on the golf tour. Walking to the first tee is in no way comparable to walking through the jungle in combat."

LARRY NELSON, from *Golf Digest*

●

"When miracles happen on the golf course, it is important to know how to respond to them. Songwriter Hoagy Carmichael, an avid golfer, once teed up on a par-three hole, picked up a club and hit the ball. It bounced once on the green, hit the pin and dropped in for a hole in one. Hoagy didn't say a word, but took another ball from his pocket, teed up, then observed, "I think I've got the idea now."

BUDDY HACKET, from *The Truth About Golf and Other Lies*

"WOW! WHEN YOU HOOK — YOU HOOK!"

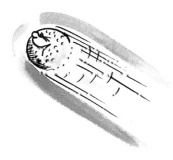

Talk to the ball. "This isn't going to hurt a bit," I tell the ball under my breath. "Sambo is just going to give you a nice little ride."

SAM SNEAD, from *The Education of a Golfer*, 1962

●

"Golf is ninety percent inspiration and ten percent perspiration."

JOHNNY MILLER

●

"I DON'T LIKE GOLFING JOKES. I'M QUITE OFTEN BEATEN BY THEM!"

"Golf is the only game where the worst player gets the best of it. They obtain more out of it with regard to both exercise and enjoyment. The good player gets worried over the slightest mistake, whereas the poor player makes too many mistakes to worry over them."

LLOYD GEORGE

"I know I'm getting better at golf because I'm hitting fewer spectators."

GERALD R. FORD

●

At the age of fifty-seven: "The fairways get longer and the holes get smaller."

BOBBY LOCKE

"NORMALLY, THAT'S A GOOD SHOT, BUT CONSIDERING THE FACT THAT YOU HIT IT, IT'S A BRILLIANT SHOT."

Victim lulled off guard and drawn into some serious-money betting, the golf hustler snicked into top gear and started playing like a master. Aware of the dupe's suspicion, the hustler feigned surprise at his miraculously improved form, shrugged modestly and muttered, "Somebody up there must like me . . ."

"Good," snapped the burly sucker, fingering his driver in a meaning manner, "because if I lose, you're likely to meet Him."

●

"I never pray on the golf course. Actually, the Lord answers my prayers everywhere except on the course."

REV. BILLY GRAHAM

●

"If I died… it meant I couldn't play golf. No way was I giving up golf, so I gave up drinking.

BOB HOPE

●

If golf is a rich man's game, why are there so many poor players?

●

Leading in the British Open, 1964: "Class, someone once said, is the ability to undergo pressure with grace. So what did I do? I just did what comes naturally. I vomited."

CHARLES PRICE, from *Golfer-At-Large*

"In prehistoric times, cavemen had a custom of beating the ground with clubs and uttering spine-chilling cries. Anthropologists call this a form of primitive self-expression. When modern men go through the same ritual, they call it golf."

HERBERT V. PROCHNOW & HERBERT V. PROCHNOW JNR.